- Annihilation of Caste by Dr B.R. Ambedkar
  Social Science, ISBN: 9789390492732

- Believe in Yourself by Joseph Murphy
  Self-Help/Motivational, ISBN: 9789388118385

- How I Made $2,000,000 in the Stock Market by Nicolas Darvas
  Self-Help, ISBN: 9789389716283

- How to Attract Money by Joseph Murphy
  Self-Help, ISBN: 9789388118408

- How to Enjoy Your Life and Your Job by Dale Carnegie
  Self-Help, ISBN: 9789387669017

- How to Stop Worrying and Start Living by Dale Carnegie
  Self-Help, ISBN: 9789380914817

- How to Win Friends and Influence People by Dale Carnegie
  Self-Help, ISBN: 9788180320217

- Jail Diary and Other Writings by Bhagat Singh
  Biographies & Memoirs, ISBN: 9789390492398

- Know Your Worth by NK Sondhi & Vibha Malhotra
  Self-Help/Motivational, ISBN: 9788180320231

- Meditations by Marcus Aurelius
  Philosophy, ISBN: 9789388118736

- My Experiments with Truth by Mahatma Gandhi
  Biographies & Memoirs, ISBN: 9789387669291

- My Inventions: The Autobiography of Nikola Tesla
  Biographies & Memoirs, ISBN: 9789388118132

Search the book by its ISBN

BESTSELLING NON-FICTION

- Relativity by Albert Einstein
  Science/Physics, ISBN: 9789380914220

- Reminiscences of a Stock Operator by Edwin Lefevre
  Business/Stock Market, ISBN: 9788194764816

- Success Through a Positive Mental Attitude by Napoleon Hill
  Self-Help, ISBN: 9789390492435

- The Art of War by Sun Tzu
  Self-Help, ISBN: 9789380914893

- The Autobiography of a Yogi by Paramahansa Yogananda
  Biographies & Memoirs, ISBN: 9789380914602

- The Diary of a Young Girl by Anne Frank
  Biographies & Memoirs, ISBN: 9789380914312

- The Elements of Style by William Strunk
  Non-Fiction, ISBN: 9789389157123

- The Law of Success by Napoleon Hill
  Self-Help, ISBN: 9788180320927

- The Power of Your Subconscious Mind by Joseph Murphy
  Self-Help, ISBN: 9788180320958

- The Richest Man in Babylon by George S. Clason
  Business & Economics, ISBN: 9789387669369

- The Science of Getting Rich by Wallace D. Wattles
  Self-Help, ISBN: 9788180320972

- The World as I See It by Albert Einstein
  Non-Fiction, ISBN: 9789388118125

51 MUST KNOW FACTS ABOUT

ALBERT EINSTEIN

GENERAL PRESS

Published by

GENERAL PRESS

4805/24, Fourth Floor, Krishna House
Ansari Road, Daryaganj, New Delhi - 110002
Ph : 011-23282971, 45795759
E-mail : generalpressindia@gmail.com

www.generalpress.in

First Edition : 2022

ISBN : 9789354991486

Published by Azeem Ahmad Khan for General Press

Contents

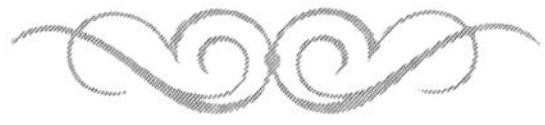

Introduction

Albert Einstein was one of the best ingenious scientists and masterminds in human history. A century ago, his remarkable published theory of General Relativity created new ideas related to the evolution of the universe and black holes, altered our knowledge of gravity, time and space dramatically. The physicist's equation that helped explain special relativity $E = MC^2$ is eminent even among those who do not understand its underlying physics.

Einstein received the Nobel Prize for Physics in the year 1921. He received the coveted prize for his explanation of the photoelectric effect and not on his ideas of relativity as then they were considered questionable, though during his acceptance speech, Einstein still opted to speak about relativity. He also tried in vain to unify all the forces of the universe in a single theory, or a theory of everything, which he was still working on at the time of his death. His extraordinary brilliant mind was advanced with creativity and allowed him to see possibilities, not limitations. He was also fuelled by an unquenchable thirst to discover, explore and indulge his curiosity. His wisdom has never been more pertinent to entrepreneurs, creators and innovators.

After his death, while performing the autopsy, Princeton pathologist Thomas Harvey extracted the scientist's brain and kept it aside in the hope of unlocking the secrets of his genius. Later, after he was able to get approval of Einstein's son, Harvey chopped the brain into pieces and sent it to various scientists for research. In the year 1999, a team from a Canadian University published a paper declaring Einstein possessed unusual folds on his parietal lobe, a part of the brain that is associated with mathematical and spatial ability.

51 Must Know Facts about Albert Einstein will take you on a journey to the life of the most prolific influencer of the 20th Century. Comprehend on the Brainiac that Einstein was, his profound life, and his incredible discoveries that contributed effectively to the world we live in today.

51
MUST KNOW FACTS ABOUT ALBERT EINSTEIN

1

Einstein didn't start speaking until the age of 3 or 4. When he did, his first sentence was to complain at dinner that the soup was too hot. When asked why he hadn't spoken before then, he replied: "because up to now, everything was in order."

2

Einstein was born on March 14, 1879, in Ulm, Württemberg, Germany. He grew up in a secular Jewish family. His father, Hermann Einstein, was a salesman and engineer who, with his brother, founded Elektrotechnische Fabrik J. Einstein & Cie, a Munich-based company that mass-produced electrical equipment. Einstein's mother, the former Pauline Koch, ran the family household. Einstein had one sister, Maja, born two years after him.

3

Up until he was 9, Einstein would think through what he wanted to say before speaking. He preferred to practice his sentences in his head or under his breath until he got them right.

4

Einstein was born with what his family thought was an abnormally oversized head. The doctor was able to convince them that his body would catch up. Once it did, his grandmother complained to his parents he was too fat.

5

Einstein attended elementary school at the Luitpold Gymnasium in Munich. However, he felt alienated there and struggled with the institution's rigid pedagogical style. He also had what were considered speech challenges, though he developed a passion for classical music and playing the violin, which would stay with him into his later years. Most consequently, Einstein's youth was marked by deep inquisitiveness and inquiry.

6

Einstein was a talented violinist. He began music lessons at the age of 5, but fell in love with music when he discovered Mozart's violin sonatas at the age of 13. His violin was nicknamed "Lina", and he said that the most joy in his life came from his violin.

7

Some researchers claimed that Einstein had a mild manifestation of autism or Asperger's syndrome.

8

At the age of 15, Einstein's refusal to bend to the authority of one of his teachers led to him being kicked out of class. In college, he irritated his professors with his impertinence, never hiding the fact that he found their classes boring.

9

Einstein would write in his memoirs that two "wonders" deeply affected his early years, according to Hans-Josef Küpper, an Albert Einstein scholar. Young Einstein encountered his first wonder—a compass—at the age of 5: He was mystified that invisible forces could deflect the needle. This would lead to a lifelong fascination with unseen forces. The second wonder came at the age of 12 when he discovered a book of geometry, which he worshipped, calling it his "holy geometry book."

10

Towards the end of the 1880s, Max Talmud, a Polish medical student who sometimes dined with the Einstein family, became an informal tutor to young Einstein. Talmud had introduced his pupil to a children's science text that inspired Einstein to dream about the nature of light. Thus, during his teens, Einstein penned what would be seen as his first major paper, "The Investigation of the State of Aether in Magnetic Fields."

11

Hermann Einstein relocated the family to Milan, Italy, in the mid-1890s after his business lost out on a major contract. Einstein was left at a relative's boarding house in Munich to complete his schooling at the Luitpold Gymnasium. Faced with military duty when he turned of age, Einstein allegedly withdrew from classes, using a doctor's note to excuse himself and claim nervous exhaustion. With their son rejoining them in Italy, his parents understood Einstein's perspective but were concerned about his future prospects as a school dropout and draft dodger.

12

Einstein was not actually a poor student. He never "failed math." At age 16, he failed his entrance exam to the Federal Polytechnic School in Zurich, but only because he struggled with the non-science subjects (especially French). Einstein continued to study and was able to attend the school the following year.

13

After graduating, Einstein faced major challenges in terms of finding academic positions, having alienated some professors over not attending class more regularly in lieu of studying independently. Einstein eventually found steady work in 1902 after receiving a referral for a clerk position in a Swiss patent office. While working at the patent office, Einstein had the time to further explore ideas that had taken hold during his studies at the Swiss Federal Institute of Technology and thus cemented his theorems on what would be known as the principle of relativity.

14

In 1905—seen by many as a "miracle year" for the theorist—Einstein had four papers published in the *Annalen der Physik*, one of the best-known physics journals of the era. Two focused on the photoelectric effect and Brownian motion. The two others, which outlined $E=MC^2$ and the special theory of relativity, were defining Einstein's career and the course of the study of physics.

15

Einstein was eventually able to gain admission into the Swiss Federal Institute of Technology in Zurich, specifically due to his superb mathematics and physics scores on the entrance exam. He was still required to complete his pre-university education first, and thus attended a high school in Aarau, Switzerland helmed by Jost Winteler. Einstein lived with the schoolmaster's family and fell in love with Winteler's daughter, Marie. Einstein later renounced his German citizenship and became a Swiss citizen at the dawn of the new century.

16

Einstein was the first to discover the equation that showed the universe is expanding, but he thought it was a mistake. Years later, Hubble's telescope confirmed that the theory of relativity was correct, and his biggest blunder was thinking he was wrong!

17

Einstein married Mileva Maric on January 6, 1903. While attending school in Zurich, Einstein met Maric, a Serbian physics student. Einstein continued to grow closer to Maric, but his parents were strongly against the relationship due to her ethnic background. Nonetheless, Einstein continued to see her, with the two developing a correspondence via letters in which he expressed many of his scientific ideas. Einstein's father passed away in 1902, and the couple married shortly thereafter. That same year the couple had a daughter, Lieserl, who might have been later raised by Maric's relatives or given up for adoption. Her ultimate fate and whereabouts remain a mystery. The couple had two sons, Hans Albert Einstein (who became a well-known hydraulic engineer) and Eduard "Tete" Einstein (who was diagnosed with schizophrenia as a young man).

18

The Einstein's marriage would not be a happy one, with the two divorcing in 1919 and Maric having an emotional breakdown in connection to the split. During his marriage to Maric, Einstein had also begun an affair some time earlier with a cousin, Elsa Löwenthal. The couple wed in 1919, the same year of Einstein's divorce. He would continue to see other women throughout his second marriage, which ended with Löwenthal's death in 1936.

19

Einstein played around with an alternative to the big bang theory. The theory proposed that the universe expanded steadily and eternally instead of all at once in a big bang. Einstein later abandoned the theory, and the paper was never published.

20

Einstein paid his wife Mileva his entire prize money from his Nobel Prize, a staggering $32,250 which was vastly more than a professor's salary back then.

21

In 1921, Einstein won the Nobel Prize for Physics for his explanation of the photoelectric effect, since his ideas on relativity were still considered questionable. He wasn't actually given the award until the following year due to a bureaucratic ruling, and during his acceptance speech, he still opted to speak about relativity.

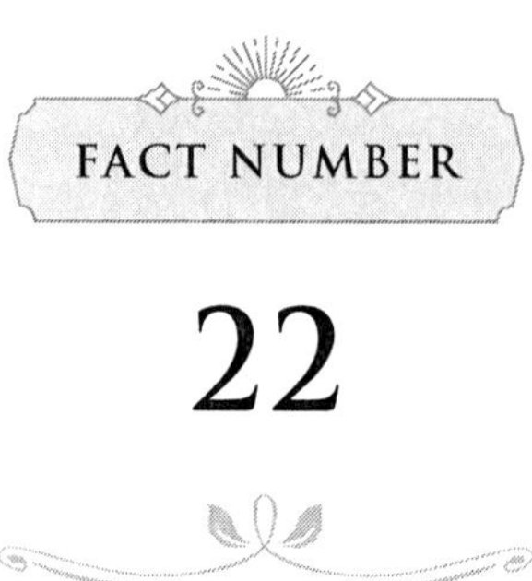

22

As a physicist, Einstein had many discoveries, but he is perhaps best known for his theory of relativity and the equation $E=MC^2$, which foreshadowed the development of atomic power and the atomic bomb.

23

Fearing a German nuclear bomb, Einstein wrote a letter to President Roosevelt encouraging him to work on a nuclear weapon. This led to the creation of the Manhattan project, which was responsible for the atomic bomb. His famous equation $E = MC^2$ also made the bomb theoretically possible.

24

Einstein first proposed a special theory of relativity in 1905 in his paper, "On the Electrodynamics of Moving Bodies," taking physics in an electrifying new direction. By November 1915, Einstein completed the general theory of relativity. Einstein considered this theory the culmination of his life research. He was convinced of the merits of general relativity because it allowed for a more accurate prediction of planetary orbits around the sun, which fell short in Isaac Newton's theory, and for a more expansive, nuanced explanation of how gravitational forces worked. Einstein's assertions were affirmed via observations and measurements by British astronomers Sir Frank Dyson and Sir Arthur Eddington during the 1919 solar eclipse, and thus a global science icon was born.

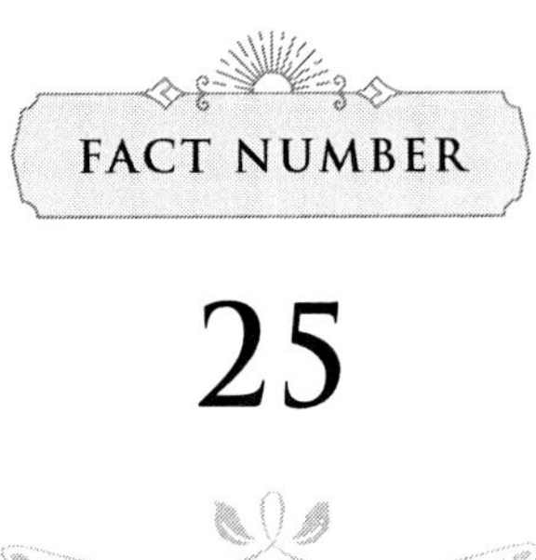

25

Formulated by Albert Einstein in 1905, the theory of relativity is the notion that the laws of physics are the same everywhere. The theory explains the behavior of objects in space and time, and it can be used to predict everything from the existence of black holes, to light bending due to gravity, to the behavior of the planet Mercury in its orbit.

26

His great breakthroughs came from experiments performed in his head rather than in the lab. Einstein performed thought experiments. At a young age, he tried to picture in his mind, what it would be like to ride alongside the light beam.

27

Einstein's 1905 paper on the matter/energy relationship proposed the equation $E=MC^2$: the energy of a body (E) is equal to the mass (M) of that body times the speed of light squared (C2). This equation suggested that tiny particles of matter could be converted into huge amounts of energy, a discovery that heralded atomic power.

28

Einstein believed in God. He defined God in an objective fashion but believed that God's work is reflected in the 'harmony of nature's laws and the beauty of all that exists.

29

Albert Einstein was known as the "people's scientist" because of his pragmatic sense of humour and his approachable manner. His hair was always uncombed, clothing scruffy, and he never wore socks—not even when visiting President Roosevelt at the White House.

30

In 1952, Albert Einstein was offered the chance to be President of Israel. He turned down the offer insisting that he was unqualified.

31

Einstein started a small discussion group called 'The Olympia Academy,' with some of his friends to discuss science and philosophy while he was unemployed. He came up with the theory of relativity at around this time.

32

Einstein loved to smoke. He believed that pipe smoking "contributes to a somewhat calm and objective judgment in all human affairs." He gave up smoking on doctor's instructions, but didn't give up the pipes themselves. He would often stick one into his mouth and chew on it.

33

Einstein loved to sail. His boat was called "Tinef" which is Yiddish for worthless or junk, and it equally described his sailing skills. Not only was he a lousy sailor, but he didn't even know how to swim!

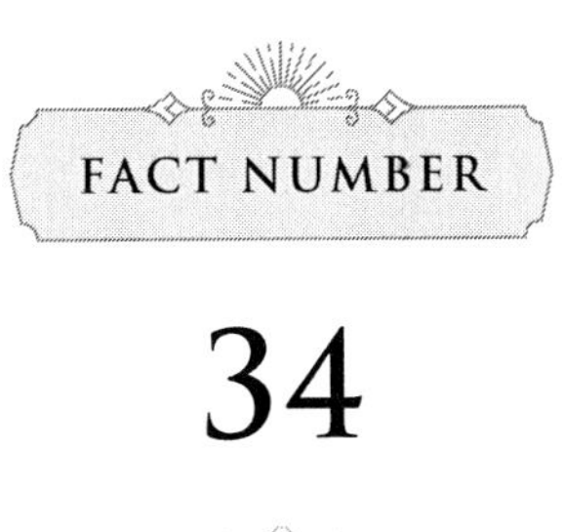

34

Einstein's brain was overall smaller than average, but the parietal lobes were 15% wider than normal. These areas are linked to mathematical ability, and visual and spatial awareness. Researchers believe that this is why Einstein tackled scientific thought the way he did.

35

As he left his 72nd birthday party, Einstein was surrounded by photographers. Tired of fake smiling, he stuck his tongue out instead. Einstein ordered 9 pictures for personal use, and signed one of them for a reporter. That photograph sold at an auction for $74,324!

36

Einstein never had a car of his own, and he never learned to drive. If he needed to go somewhere by car, he had friends or a chauffeur drove him.

37

In December of 1932, the FBI started keeping a file on Einstein. At the time of his death, the file was 1427 pages long. Then FBI director J. Edgar Hoover was deeply suspicious of Einstein, and believed he was an extreme radical and a communist.

38

Towards the end of WWII, Einstein had a passionate affair with Margarita Konenkova – a brilliant scientist and Russian spy. Their affair only ended when she and her husband returned to Moscow in 1945. Konenkova was allegedly tasked with learning about and "influencing" the American nuclear program, and was instructed to get close to J. Robert Oppenheimer of the Manhattan Project. Einstein was not directly involved in the Manhattan Project, so it's not entirely clear what Konenkova was hoping to get out of him.

39

Einsteinium is the 99th element on the periodic table. It's named after Albert Einstein, though he actually had nothing to do with its discovery or research.

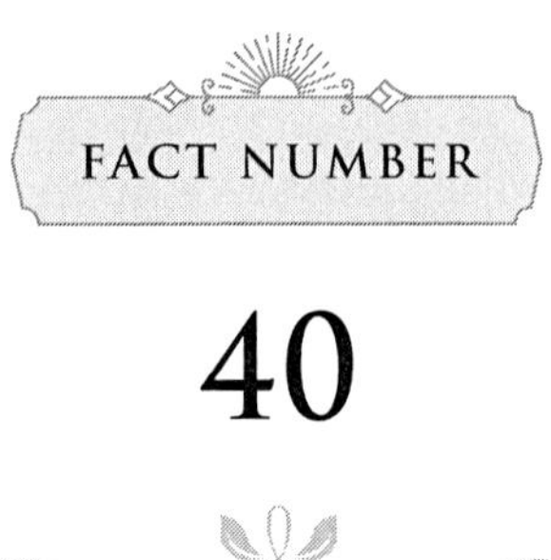

40

After moving to the United States, Einstein became an active member of the NAACP (National Association for the Advancement of Colored People), and courageously took a public stand against racial segregation in America.

41

In 1923, Einstein travelled to Jerusalem to present the first scientific address at the Hebrew University he had helped to fund. At one of his speaking engagements, he declared: "I consider this the greatest day of my life".

42

Einstein's wife Elsa managed his fan mail and collected $1.00 for an autograph and $5.00 for a photograph. Einstein donated the proceeds to charity.

43

Einstein tirelessly wrote letters to Presidents, prime ministers, and other leaders asking them to take in unemployed German-Jewish scientists during the Nazi regime. His letters saved over 1,000 Jews from persecution and the Nazi camps. He also wrote a now-famous letter to FDR shortly before figuring out uranium-powered nuclear chain reactions, which would power the atomic bombs.

44

After the US dropped the atomic bomb on Hiroshima and Nagasaki in 1945, Einstein became active in the political movement to prevent the use of atomic bombs in the future.

45

A Nazi magazine in Germany printed an enemies list, and Einstein was on it listed as "Not Yet Hanged." It also offered a $5000 Bounty for his head.

46

Einstein realized his life was at risk after Hitler assumed power in Germany. Einstein fled to Belgium, where he learned that his boat and cottage had been seized. He then escaped to England, and he was kept under armed protection until he found safety in America.

47

Einstein said: "If a cluttered desk is a sign of a cluttered mind, of what, then, is an empty desk a sign?" A famous photograph taken on the day he died showed bulging book shelves, a desk cluttered with notebooks, journals, a pipe & a tobacco tin.

48

Right before he died, Einstein uttered his final words to a nurse. Unfortunately, the words were spoken in German—a language the nurse didn't speak or understand.

49

Einstein died of an aortic aneurysm on April 18, 1955. A blood vessel burst near his heart, according to the American Museum of Natural History (AMNH). When asked if he wanted to have surgery, Einstein refused. "I want to go when I want to go," he said. "It is tasteless to prolong life artificially. I have done my share; it is time to go. I will do it elegantly."

50

Einstein had a terrible memory for details he deemed unimportant. When questioned about why he had to look up his phone number, Einstein replied: "Why should I memorize something I can so easily get from a book?"

51

Einstein's body—most of it, anyway—was cremated; his ashes were spread in an undisclosed location, according to the AMNH. However, a doctor at Princeton Hospital, Thomas Harvey, had performed an autopsy, apparently without permission, and removed Einstein's brain and eyeballs, according to Matt Blitz, who wrote about Einstein's brain in a 2015 column for Today I Found Out.

OTHER TITLES IN THIS SERIES

51 Must Know Facts About **Anne Frank**

51 Must Know Facts About **Blood**

51 Must Know Facts About **Brain**

51 Must Know Facts About **Diabetes**

51 Must Know Facts About **Heart**

51 Must Know Facts About **Human Body**

51 Must Know Facts About **Islam**

51 Must Know Facts About **Lungs**

51 Must Know Facts About **Pregnancy**

51 Must Know Facts About **Thomas Alva Edison**

Search the book by its ISBN

OTHER BOOKS YOU MAY LIKE

- 1984 by George Orwell, ISBN: 9789380914947
- 12 Years a Slave by Solomon Northup, ISBN: 9789390492374
- 51 Most Powerful Prayers by Ryan, ISBN: 9789354990847
- A Christmas Carol by Charles Dickens, ISBN: 9788193545874
- A Cloud by Day, a Fire by Night by AW Tozer, ISBN: 9789354990854
- A Passage to India by E.M. Forster, ISBN: 9789354990205
- A Room of One's Own by Virginia Woolf, ISBN: 9789354990281
- A Streetcar Named Desire by Tennessee Williams, ISBN: 9788194748601
- A Wrinkle in Time by Madeleine L'Engle, ISBN: 9789354991066
- Abraham Lincoln by Lord Charnwood, ISBN: 9789380914251
- Absolute Surrender by Andrew Murray, ISBN: 9789389716269
- Animal Farm by George Orwell, ISBN: 9789380914701
- Anthem by Ayn Rand, ISBN: 9789389157079
- As a Man Thinketh by James Allen, ISBN: 9788180320262
- As I Lay Dying by William Faulkner, ISBN: 9789390492381
- Awakened Imagination by Neville Goddard, ISBN: 9789389157086
- Be What You Wish by Neville Goddard, ISBN: 9789387669550
- Chanakya Neeti by Chanakya, ISBN: 9789389716276
- Civilization and Its Discontents by Sigmund Freud, ISBN: 9789387669499
- Delighting in God by AW Tozer, ISBN: 9788194748632
- Demian by Hermann Hesse, ISBN: 9789387669567
- Experiencing the Holy Spirit by Andrew Murray, ISBN: 9788194764809
- Feeling is the Secret by Neville Goddard, ISBN: 9789389157109
- George Orwell Combo : Animal Farm & 1984, ISBN: 9789390492459
- Gravity by George Gamow, ISBN: 9789388118484
- Guerrilla Warfare by Ernesto Che Guevara, ISBN: 9789354990366

Develop your reading habit | **Gift books to your friends**

OTHER BOOKS YOU MAY LIKE

- The Magic of Faith by Joseph Murphy, ISBN: 9789388118743
- The Miracles of Your Mind by Joseph Murphy, ISBN: 9788180320743
- The Mysterious Affair at Styles by Agatha Christie, ISBN: 9789390492510
- The Origin of Species by Charles Darwin, ISBN: 9788180320453
- The Plague by Albert Camus, ISBN: 9788194764892
- The Power of Awareness by Neville Goddard, ISBN: 9789387669406
- The Power of Positive Thinking by Norman Vincent Peale, ISBN: 9789388118569
- The Problem of Increasing Human Energy by Nikola Tesla, ISBN: 9789354990953
- The Prophet by Kahlil Gibran, ISBN: 9789380914022
- The Psychopathology of Everyday Life by Sigmund Freud, ISBN: 9789388118071
- The Pursuit of God by AW Tozer, ISBN: 9789389157147
- The Railway Children by E Nesbit, ISBN: 9789354990960
- The Red Badge of Courage by Stephen Crane, ISBN: 9789354990977
- The Sound and the Fury by William Faulkner, ISBN: 9789390492572
- The Stranger by Albert Camus, ISBN: 9789390492589
- The Sun Also Rises by Ernest Hemingway, ISBN: 9789354990984
- The Yoga Sutras of Patanjali by Patanjali, ISBN: 9789389716351
- Their Eyes Were Watching God by Zora Neale Hurston, ISBN: 9788194764885
- Think and Grow Rich by Napoleon Hill, ISBN: 9788180320255
- Thought Vibration by William Walker Atkinson, ISBN: 9789389157154
- To the Lighthouse by Virginia Woolf, ISBN: 9789390492190
- Who were the Shudras by Dr B.R. Ambedkar, ISBN: 9789354991028
- World's Best Short Stories: Volume 1 by Various Authors, ISBN: 9789390492275
- Wuthering Heights by Emily Brontë, ISBN: 9788193545898
- Your Faith is Your Fortune by Neville Goddard, ISBN: 9789389157161
- Zen in the Art of Archery by Eugen Herrigel, ISBN: 9789354991059

Develop your reading habit | **Gift books to your friends**